DIRECTORY

ON THE

CANONICAL STATUS
OF THE CLERGY

RIGHTS, OBLIGATIONS
AND PROCEDURES

Approved for publication by the
Catholic Bishops' Conference of England and Wales

CATHOLIC TRUTH SOCIETY
PUBLISHERS TO THE HOLY SEE

Directory on the Canonical Status of the Clergy: Published 2009 by the Incorporated Catholic Truth Society, 40-46 Harleyford Road, London, SE11 5AY Tel: 020 7640 0042 Fax: 020 7640 0046. Copyright © 2009 The Catholic Bishops' Conference of England and Wales. References in the Directory are to the *Code of Canon Law*, Copyright © English Translation 1983, 1997 The Canon Law Society Trust. Original Latin Text © Copyright 1983 Libreria Editrice Vaticana, Vatican City.

website: www.cts-online.org.uk

ISBN 978 1 86082 576 7

Contents

Introduction 5
1. Aims 9

Part One: Canonical Provisions Concerning Clerics

2. Formation and Admission to Ordination. 19
3. Incardination. 21
4. Rights of the Clergy 24
5. Obligations of the Clergy 26
6. Financial Provision 29
7. Absence 32
8. The Power of Governance of the
   Diocesan Bishop. 34
9. Appointment to Ecclesiastical Office 40
10. Resignation from Ecclesiastical Office 42
11. Medical Examination and
    Psychological Assessment. 44

Part Two: Processes

12. Confidentiality 49
13. Removal from Ecclesiastical Office. 50
14. Removal of Parish Priests 53
15. Transfer from Ecclesiastical Office 59
16. Transfer of Parish Priests. 61
17. Disciplinary Penal Offences and Sanctions. 64
18. Disciplinary Penal Process 67
19. Temporary Withdrawal from Active Ministry 81
20. Administrative Recourse. 85
21. Dispute Resolution 87

Appendix 1: Definition of Terms. 92
Appendix 2: Checklist for Diocesan Handbooks 94

Introduction

The aim of this Directory is to set out and draw together the relevant canons which establish the rights and obligations of the clergy, and to provide a clear presentation of the canonical processes which affect them. In the Preface to the 1983 *Code of Canon Law*, we read that: "Pastors have at their disposal secure norms by which they may correctly direct the exercise of the sacred ministry. To each person is given a source of knowing his or her own proper rights and duties. Arbitrariness in acting can be precluded...". It is my hope that this Directory will provide that "source of knowing", together with a clarity and transparency within which we may all be able to familiarise ourselves more readily with those rights and duties most directly connected with our canonical "status" as clerics and holders of ecclesiastical office.

Alongside the provisions of the Code, there are some proposed developments in respect of disciplinary and administrative matters which may be helpful. These sections are printed in *italics*, to make it clear that they are not contained in the Code itself. Provision of a procedure to resolve administrative disputes was contemplated for the revised Code, but in the end the Code Commission decided to leave to Conferences of Bishops the decision as to whether to introduce administrative tribunals or similar bodies according to local need. "Although it is very much to be desired that administrative tribunals be regularly established by Conferences of Bishops, for promoting subjective rights and for ordering administrative justice better, it does not seem opportune to impose such a burden by universal law... and therefore it seems appropriate to move gradually and in some way voluntarily, according to local possibilities and sources." (Com.CIC Rec, *"Acta Commissionis: Relatio"*, Comm 16 (1984) 85-86).

The rights and obligations of clergy contained in the Code are set in an ecclesial context which informs their meaning and understanding. In the words of Pope John Paul II: "The code is in no way intended as a substitute for faith, grace, charisms and especially charity in the life of the Church and of the faithful. On the contrary, its purpose is to create such an order in the ecclesial society that, while assigning primacy to love, grace and charisms, it at the same time renders their organic development easier in the life of both the ecclesial society and in the individual persons who belong to it." (*Sacrae disciplinae leges*, 25th January 1983)

This Directory was approved for publication by the plenary meeting of the Bishops' Conference of England and Wales in November 2008. The resolution passed unanimously at that meeting stated that: "The Bishops' Conference commends the *Directory on the Canonical Status of the Clergy* as a clear statement of the canonical norms regarding the rights and obligations of clergy, and in setting out good practice in their interpretation and implementation."

I hope this Directory will be a useful reference work for those not expert in canon law, and that it will provide a clear guide to the rights and obligations of the clergy, and provide for our Dioceses appropriate processes to be tried *"ad experimentum"* in the resolution of disciplinary and administrative conflicts. It is intended that it will act as a clear and common standard for the development of Handbooks in each Diocese.

Finally, I want to express my gratitude and thanks to all the members of the Working Group who put this document together in consultation with the Diocesan Bishops and clergy of England and Wales, and in particular Ed Morgan and Fr Kristian Paver who did the bulk of the work involved. We are also very grateful to the Congregation for Clergy for their helpful comments on the draft text.

Archbishop Peter Smith
Vice President
Catholic Bishops' Conference of England and Wales
May 2009

1. AIMS

1.1 From the earliest times, the life and ministry of priests and deacons, under the guidance and leadership of the bishops, has been central to the mission of the Church. The relationship between priests and deacons and their bishops is a unique one, which cannot be fully comprehended in solely juridical terms. Addressing this relationship, St Ignatius of Antioch writes: "That is why it is proper for your conduct and your practices to correspond closely with the mind of the bishop. And this, indeed, they are doing; your justly respected clergy, who are a credit to God, are attuned to their bishop like the strings of a harp, and the result is a hymn of praise to Jesus Christ from minds that are in unison, and affections that are in harmony"[1].

1.2 To assist the clergy in understanding the juridical implications of this relationship, the aim of this Directory is to bring together in a systematic and accessible way the provisions of the *Code of Canon Law* concerning the rights and obligations of clerics

---

[1] St Ignatius of Antioch, *Epistle to the Ephesians*, paragraph 4.

and the canonical procedures which are necessary to maintain discipline and ensure the just resolution of disputes.

1.3 Mindful of its aims, this Directory does not in any way replace the provisions of the Code itself, which must remain the sole reference point for any canonical action, interpretation or application. As a result, if there is any conflict between the contents of the Directory and the canons of the Code, the Code always prevails.

1.4 As with all law in the Church, the context for the correct understanding and application of the contents of this Directory is to be found in the theological and spiritual principles which underpin it. Reference should therefore be had to other magisterial sources, especially the *Directory on the Life and Ministry of Priests*[2] and the *Directory for the Life and Ministry of Permanent Deacons*[3], which synthesize much of the Church's doctrine, particularly in the light of the Second Vatican Council and in the recent

---

[2] Congregation for the Clergy, *Directory on the Ministry and Life of Priests*, 31st January 1994.

[3] Congregation for the Clergy, *Directory for the Ministry and Life of Permanent Deacons*, 22nd February 1998.

Magisterium of the Roman Pontiffs, concerning the nature, ministry, duties and rights of priests and deacons. This magisterial teaching will provide a rich ecclesial basis for, and avoid an excessively legalistic and individualistic interpretation of the relationship between the Diocesan Bishop and his clergy.

1.5 Within the context of England and Wales, the common law has long recognised that a cleric does not enjoy the status of an employee[4]. Traditionally, ministers of religion have been viewed as "office holders"[5]. This is in no small part due to the spiritual nature of the duties undertaken by them[6]. The Church has continuously held that the relationship between

---

[4] The principal employment protection legislation proceeds on this basis. Cf Section 230 of the Employment Rights Act 1996.

[5] President of the Methodist Conference v Parfitt [1984] IRLR 141, [1984] ICR 176 CA.

[6] Whilst the established principle that ministers of religion are not bound by a contract of employment has been upheld, in two recent judgements (Percy v Church of Scotland Board of National Mission [2005] UKHL 73 and The New Testament Church of God v Stewart [2007] EWCA Civ 1004), it has been decided that the absence of an intention to create legal relationships between a Church and one of its ministers cannot be presumed, but must be shown from a careful analysis of the particular doctrine and discipline of each Church. It is the firmly-held and constant position of the Catholic Church that its teaching and understanding of the ordained ministry absolutely precludes an intention to create legal relationships akin to employment.

a bishop and his clergy is in no way comparable to that of an employer and his employees[7].

1.6 The Catholic understanding of ecclesial communion, ordained ministry and hierarchy have little in common with the secular workplace and its management structures. In addition, within the Particular Church, one is required to apply the universal laws of the Church, laws intended to safeguard and promote ecclesial identity, matters of doctrine and the Church's mission. As a consequence, there is little scope for the wholesale adoption of standards or protocols formulated and applied in the secular context. Where possible, developments in notions of best practice have been considered in the compilation of this Directory, except where such practices would be contrary to the Church's universal laws.

1.7 In some cases, this Directory may prompt the clergy to a deeper awareness of canon law and its role within the Church community. It is also recognised that for

---

[7] Pontifical Council for Legislative Texts, Explanatory Note: *Elements to establish the area of canonical responsibility of the diocesan Bishop towards clerics incardinated within the diocese and who exercise a ministry within it*, 12th February 2004, *Communicationes* 36(2004)33-38.

others, the detail of the Code may, by reason of their own personal circumstances, be less familiar[8]. The hope and aim of this Directory is to provide clarity and transparency within which each is able to more readily familiarise himself with those rights and duties most directly connected with his status as a cleric and holder of ecclesiastical office.

1.8 This Directory is primarily concerned with, and intended for the use of, the secular clergy. Whilst matters relating to penal processes are governed by universal law and the Diocesan Bishop exercises jurisdiction over religious clergy in matters concerning the care of souls, the public exercise of divine worship and other works of the apostolate[9], religious clergy and clergy belonging to Societies of Apostolic Life are subject in all other matters to the Rule and Constitutions[10] of the Institute into which they are incardinated.

1.9 This Directory does not include policies and procedures specifically related to the safeguarding of

---

[8] All clergy are bound to acquire knowledge of the sacred sciences so as to better perform their priestly duties [can 279§3].

[9] can 678§1.

[10] can 587.

children and vulnerable adults. For these, reference should be had to the National Catholic Safeguarding Commission and the Catholic Safeguarding Advisory Service[11]. However, inasmuch as these policies and procedures touch upon the general provisions of canon law dealt with in this Directory, there will be an occasional point of convergence.

1.10 Apart from the processes taken directly from the Code, a number of provisions in the Directory concerning the rights and obligations of the clergy require further development and application at the level of each Particular Church. Therefore, it is expected that each Diocesan Bishop will need to produce a Handbook for his own clergy to complement this Directory, having particular regard to those issues highlighted as requiring more detailed treatment in Diocesan Handbooks[12]. Where such Handbooks already exist, they may need to be revised.

1.11 Given the need to respond to changing and new circumstances, as well as a result of experience

---

[11] The current safeguarding policies and procedures are now helpfully brought together online and can be found at *www.csasprocedures.uk.net*.

[12] See appendix 2.

arising from the implementation of these provisions, it is foreseen that this Directory and Diocesan Handbooks will be subject to periodic review.

Part One:

Canonical Provisions Concerning Clerics

2. Formation and Admission to Ordination

2.1 The Church enjoys the absolute right to regulate the training and suitability of those admitted to studies for the sacred ministries[13]. The process of selection, formation or assessment of those admitted to formation programmes or similar studies falls within the competence of the Diocesan Bishop and the Conference.

2.2 The fundamental principles underlying selection for sacred ministry in accordance with the doctrine of the Church can be summarised as follows:

(i) No one may be coerced into choosing a state in life[14].

(ii) No person has the right to ordination[15]. Rather, a candidate is only to be ordained where his freedom and suitability have been confirmed and the Diocesan Bishop is satisfied that his ordination is useful to the Church[16].

---

[13] can 232.

[14] cann 219, 1026.

[15] This is without prejudice to the position of transitional deacons dealt with in can 1030.

[16] can 1025§2.

(iii) Admission to the clerical state arises through ordination to the diaconate[17].

(iv) Only baptised men can validly receive ordination[18].

2.3 Through ordination a cleric makes a life-long commitment to the Church[19] and is enrolled for service within the Particular Church for which he has been ordained[20]. In the case of religious clerics the same life-long bond is made to the Institute of which they are a member. It is within and by reference to these communities that the rights and obligations of the clergy find expression.

2.4 Eligibility for ordination presupposes that a candidate is not subject to any impediment or irregularity which precludes reception of the sacrament[21].

---

[17] can 266.
[18] can 1024.
[19] can 290.
[20] can 266.
[21] can 1025§1.

3. INCARDINATION

3.1 In the Catholic understanding of ministry, all priests and deacons are bound through ordination to a Particular Church or religious institute by incardination. This bond is life-long and is the source of mutual rights and obligations between the individual cleric and his bishop or religious institute. The reasons for incardination are (a) to permit the bishop to provide effectively for the pastoral needs of his diocese; (b) to promote discipline amongst the clergy; and (c) to ensure that the spiritual and material needs of each cleric are met.

3.2 Incardination in a Particular Church or religious institute is the firm juridical basis for the life and ministry of every cleric, regardless of the work that they do. Indeed, the cleric's bishop or religious institute retains the life-long commitment to care for him spiritually and materially, although not necessarily solely from Church resources, even if the cleric is removed from pastoral ministry or incapacitated for office in any way.

3.3 The Church has long recognised the essential and fundamental character of the relationship which arises between the Diocesan Bishop (and through him the Particular Church) and the cleric. Its mandatory nature[22] serves as a recognition and reminder that the ministry of the cleric can only be exercised from a position of communion with his Bishop, as well as the nature of the rights acquired by the cleric as a member of the Particular Church.

3.4 From incardination, therefore, the following consequences arise:

(i) The cleric serves within the Particular Church according to the mandate and faculties conferred by the Diocesan Bishop.

(ii) Whilst the cleric is a co-worker of the Diocesan Bishop in the mission of the Particular Church, he is also subject to the legislative, administrative and judicial authority of the Diocesan Bishop[23].

(iii) Whilst in no sense an employee of the Diocesan Bishop, the Particular Church, through the person of the Diocesan Bishop, is bound to protect the rights of clerics within the diocese including, but not limited to, their physical welfare and material support[24].

---

[22] can 265.
[23] cann 381§1, 391§1.
[24] can 384.

3.5 From time to time, therefore, the Diocesan Bishop, in exercising his power of governance, may be required in his dealings with a particular cleric to draw upon his regulatory powers or to exercise his administrative discretion. As detailed in later sections of this Directory, these actions are subject to detailed provision within the Code. As far as possible, however, any decisions affecting the rights and position of a cleric will only be taken following appropriate consultation, particularly with the cleric himself.

4. Rights of the Clergy

4.1 A cleric enjoys rights in common with all of the faithful and in summary form these rights include:

(i) Equality of dignity and action[25].

(ii) The right to communicate his needs and concerns[26].

(iii) The right to expression of opinions concerning the good of the Church[27].

(iv) The right to freedom of inquiry and expression insofar as he is directly concerned in the sacred disciplines[28].

(v) The right to protection of his reputation from unlawful harm[29] and the right to privacy[30].

(vi) The right to vindicate his rights by way of canonical process[31].

(vii) The right to challenge the judicial and administrative decisions of the Diocesan Bishop concerning his life and ministry[32].

---

[25] can 208.

[26] can 212.

[27] can 212§3. For the conditions regarding the exercise of this right reference must be had to the relevant provisions of the Code.

[28] can 218.

[29] can 220.

[30] can 220.

[31] can 221§1.

[32] This aspect of redress is dealt with in detail in the sections dealing with processes and administrative recourse.

Rights of the Clergy 25

(viii) The right not to be punished in connection with the conduct of his ministry save in accordance with the Code[33].

4.2 Moreover, the clergy have additional rights specific to their state. These include:

(i) Financial provision[34].

(ii) Annual vacation[35].

(iii) The freedom to tender resignation from ecclesiastical office[36].

(iv) The right not to be removed from ecclesiastical office except for grave or just causes depending on the nature of the appointment[37].

---

[33] can 221§3.

[34] can 281. In the case of permanent deacons, this provision should be read in the light of can 281§3.

[35] can 283§2.

[36] can 187.

[37] can 193.

5. Obligations of Clergy

5.1 The exercise of ministry within the Church is and remains dependent upon the obligation of the clergy to maintain communion with their Bishop and to act in conformity with the Church's teachings and discipline.

5.2 Whilst a cleric by virtue of ordination is called to ministry within the Particular Church into which he is incardinated, the nature of that ministry and the authority which he exercises will depend on the particular ecclesiastical office he holds.

5.3 The obligations of the clerical state assumed by the cleric include the responsibility that he continues in the development of his own spiritual life, fostering and cultivating those aspects of conduct consistent with his calling.

5.4 It is for these reasons that the Code imposes specific obligations upon the cleric, including:

(i) To show reverence and obedience to the Supreme Pontiff and his Diocesan Bishop[38].

---

[38] can 273.

Obligations of Clergy

(ii) To maintain continence through celibacy[39].

(iii) To undertake any ecclesiastical office or function entrusted to him by the Diocesan Bishop[40].

(iv) To carry out the Liturgy of the Hours daily[41], and to engage in spiritual retreats and prayer[42].

(vi) To continue in his studies[43].

(v) Not to engage or participate in any association whose purpose or activities cannot be reconciled with the obligations of the clerical state[44].

(vi) To foster simplicity of life [45].

(vii) Not to be absent from his diocese for a considerable time except for vacation or unless he has received the permission of the Diocesan Bishop, whether expressly or otherwise[46].

(viii) To abide by norms concerning dress[47].

(ix) Not to conduct himself in a manner unbecoming to the clerical state[48].

---

[39] can 277. Certain clergy are exempt from this obligation either by the law itself or dispensation.

[40] can 274§2.

[41] In the case of permanent deacons, this obligation is subject to the direction of the Conference.

[42] can 276§2,4° and 5°.

[43] can 279.

[44] can 278§3.

[45] can 282.

[46] can 283.

[47] can 284.

[48] For the conduct anticipated in this provision see can 285.

5.5 It will be apparent that the specific obligations cited in the preceding paragraph are not exhaustive. The Code seeks to provide a framework within which the internal spiritual and intellectual development of a cleric may be afforded priority, whilst at the same time, there is a clear understanding of the need for symmetry between internal development and external action. By means of both, the benefits to be derived from a cleric's ministry and the good of the Church as a whole are safeguarded.

5.6 Moreover, a cleric is subject to additional obligations arising out of or in connection with the specific ecclesiastical office to which he is appointed[49].

---

[49] For example, those applicable to Parish Priests and Deans in can 527 and can 555 respectively.

6. Financial Provision

6.1 Since a cleric devotes himself to the service of the Church through ordination, and by reason of his incardination within the Particular Church, he deserves financial support[50]. In the case of religious clerics all necessary welfare and support is provided by their Institute.

6.2 Such support is by no means equivalent to what might otherwise be termed "wages", not least because this support is not in any way dependent upon the carrying out of active ministry within the Church. Rather, the right is directed towards ensuring that the cleric has sufficient financial means to live in a manner befitting his clerical state, whilst insulating him against the financial cost of discharging his duties.

6.3 In this respect, a fundamental distinction needs to be made between the permanent diaconate on the one hand and the transitional diaconate and the priesthood on the other. Where the former receives

---

[50] can 281.

or has received income from the exercise of a secular profession, he is to ensure that he and his family are provided for from this income. However, where such income is absent, the Diocesan Bishop shall ensure that provision is made in accordance with the Code[51].

6.4 Since the right of financial support is a manifestation of the relationship of incardination, subject to any loss of such rights, it extends for the whole of the cleric's life. Where the cleric is dismissed from the clerical state, the right to financial and material support is similarly lost[52]. However, even following dismissal, the Diocesan Bishop, mindful of his pastoral obligations, shall in the case of genuine need make provision for the former cleric[53].

6.5 Since the right to financial support is life-long, the principles concerning financial provision for those who have resigned from ecclesiastical office due to age[54] or ill-health are to be carefully set out in Diocesan Handbooks.

---

[51] can 281§3.
[52] can 292.
[53] can 1350§2.
[54] can 538§3.

Financial Provision

6.6 Where a cleric is appointed to the office of Parish Priest, he will invariably be provided with accommodation in order to carry out that office effectively. Accordingly, following removal or transfer from the office of Parish Priest, the Diocesan Bishop shall pay particular regard to the well-being of the priest[55].

6.7 The accommodation provided for clergy, particularly the use of diocesan property by those no longer holding ecclesiastical office[56], is to be carefully dealt with in Diocesan Handbooks to ensure fair and appropriate provision.

---

[55] can 1747§2.
[56] can 538§3.

7. Absence

7.1 It is the right of every cleric to take annual leave[57]. The timing of this leave should be determined having regard to the particular ecclesiastical office held by the cleric and his pastoral commitments. The duration of annual leave should not lead to the neglect of the ecclesiastical office or, in the case of those having pastoral responsibilities, the leadership and sacramental needs of the people entrusted to him[58]. Annual leave does not include those periods in which the cleric fulfils his right and duty to continue his own spiritual development by means of retreat and spiritual conferences.

7.2 *When an absence exceeds the period of one week, the appropriate diocesan official, e.g. the vicar general or the dean, is to be informed.*

7.3 *Those who are married and admitted to the clerical state shall also be entitled to further periods of absence in respect of parental leave as agreed with the Diocesan Bishop.*

---

[57] In the case of Parish Priests, this leave is dealt with in can 533§2.
[58] can 283§2.

7.4 *Periods of absence may also be granted by means of a sabbatical. Eligibility for sabbatical and its duration are subject to individual agreement between the cleric and his Diocesan Bishop. The principles on which this agreement is based should be contained in the Diocesan Handbook.*

8. The Power of Governance of the Diocesan Bishop

8.1 A diocese is a portion of the Church community entrusted to the Diocesan Bishop[59]. The Diocesan Bishop, as chief shepherd of a Particular Church, is invested with judicial, administrative and legislative power over those entrusted to his care[60], save where the law or a decree of the Supreme Pontiff provides to the contrary[61].

8.2 Within his Particular Church, the Diocesan Bishop is the successor to the Apostles. In consequence, it is incumbent upon him to show concern for all present within his diocese. He is to have a particular concern for all the clergy within his diocese, whether incardinated or not[62], in ministry or simply resident[63].

---

[59] can 369.

[60] can 391§2.

[61] can 381.

[62] If a cleric is not incardinated into the diocese in which he is living or residing, the canonical rights and duties arising from incardination remain the responsibility of the Diocesan Bishop in whose diocese the cleric is incardinated.

[63] can 384.

8.3 Whilst the clergy are juridical subjects of the Diocesan Bishop, they are also his counsellors and co-workers[64].

8.4 The power of governance[65] enjoyed by the Diocesan Bishop within his own diocese extends to issues concerning:

(i) Ecclesiastical discipline.

(ii) The administration of sacraments and celebration of the liturgy.

(iii) Catholic education.

(iv) The exercise of ministry and apostolic activity.

(v) The making of particular laws, including penal laws[66].

8.5 Since the Diocesan Bishop represents his diocese in all its juridical affairs[67], it is through the Diocesan Bishop and the proper exercise of his powers that the rights and interests of the clergy are safeguarded and realised. These include:

(i) Provision for the welfare of clerics[68].

---

[64] can 384.
[65] cann 129§1, 391§1.
[66] can 1315.
[67] can 393.
[68] can 281.

(ii) Adherence to due process in the transfer and removal of clerics[69].

(iii) The conduct of preliminary investigations concerning alleged canonical offences[70].

(iv) Compliance with the norms concerning trials and processes.

(v) The application and cessation of penalties[71].

8.6 In matters which involve the exercise of executive power, the Diocesan Bishop may call upon the assistance of a Vicar General or Episcopal Vicars. Similarly, in judicial matters his powers may be exercised through the person of a Judicial Vicar or Judges. In all matters concerning his legislative powers, however, the Diocesan Bishop must act personally[72].

8.7 The Diocesan Bishop must always exercise his power of governance in accordance with the Code, regarding both procedure and substance[73]. However,

---

[69] can 1740 and following.

[70] can 1717.

[71] cann 1341, 1343 and 1356.

[72] can 391§2.

[73] can 391§1.

he is invested with considerable discretion in the exercise of his executive authority.

8.8 *Where the exercise of this authority impacts on the rights of a cleric, it will take the form of a decree.*

8.9 The Code includes detailed provisions concerning the form and content of decrees and the process by which they might lawfully be issued. The following is a summary of the relevant principles:

(i) Before validly exercising any executive power, the Diocesan Bishop must satisfy himself that there are canonical grounds for him to do so[74].

(ii) Prior to issuing a decree the Diocesan Bishop should consult those whose rights are likely to be adversely affected.

(iii) The decree must clearly express:

i. The conduct required on the part of the cleric in order to achieve compliance.

ii. The grounds upon which the decree has been issued.

iii. The right of the cleric to administrative recourse and the manner of seeking it, with particular mention of the established time limits.

---

[74] can 50.

iv. The consequences of non-compliance[75].

(iv) The decree takes effect when communicated to the person to whom it is directed[76]. Thereafter a decree will remain in force until revoked by further decree of the same or superior authority.

8.10 *If a decree is likely to affect adversely the canonical rights of the cleric[77], prior to issuing the decree, the Diocesan Bishop shall:*

(i) *Provide written notice to the cleric likely to be adversely affected of the basis for issuing the decree, including proofs if there are any, the terms of the proposed decree and advising the parties of the right to be heard.*

(ii) *Invite the cleric to attend a meeting to be arranged at a mutually convenient time and advise them of their right to be accompanied.*

(iii) *In advance of this meeting, if he opposes the issuing of the decree, the cleric shall set out in writing his grounds of opposition and provide any evidence relied upon in support.*

---

[75] For the provisions regulating the terms of the decree see can 51.

[76] can 54.

[77] For the canonical procedures regarding the transfer of removal of Parish Priests see Sections 14 and 16.

(iv) *At the meeting provide the parties with the opportunity to challenge and/or rebut any material relied upon by the Diocesan Bishop.*

(v) *The content of this meeting shall be formally minuted and circulated for agreement between the parties within a reasonable time following its conclusion (which should not normally exceed the period of 14 days).*

(vi) *Within 30 days of this meeting, the Diocesan Bishop shall communicate his decision (together with the reasons for it) to the cleric affected.*

9. Appointment to Ecclesiastical Office

9.1 Following ordination, a cleric may be appointed to an ecclesiastical office[78]. Whilst some ecclesiastical offices may be allocated to priests alone[79], others may also be open to deacons and lay persons.

9.2 Appointment to an ecclesiastical office within his diocese falls within the free conferral of the Diocesan Bishop[80]. Admission to the clerical state does not confer any right to such an appointment.

9.3 All appointments are to be made in writing[81]. *In addition, the cleric's acceptance of the office is to be similarly recorded.*

9.4 Unless the document confirming the appointment stipulates to the contrary, or the Code expressly provides otherwise, an appointment to ecclesiastical office shall be for an indefinite period of time.

---

[78] can 145 - provided it possesses the qualities of stability and is exercised for a spiritual purpose.

[79] e.g. that of Parish Priest – can 521§1.

[80] cann 147, 157.

[81] can 156.

9.5 Once validly appointed, a cleric may only be removed from ecclesiastical office for a just or grave cause, depending of the nature of the appointment[82]. In order to ascertain the existence of such a cause, the adoption and completion of an investigation in accordance with the relevant provisions of the Code is required[83].

---

[82] can 193. A just reason is required where an office has been conferred at the prudent discretion of the Diocesan Bishop. In all other cases, a grave reason is required to remove a cleric from an ecclesiastical office.

[83] See Section 14.

10. Resignation from Ecclesiastical Office

10.1 A cleric appointed to an ecclesiastical office is required to discharge his obligations diligently. However, where the holder of the office considers there to be just cause which renders him unable to fulfil the duties of his office, he may submit his resignation to the Diocesan Bishop[84].

10.2 In order to be valid this resignation must be made in writing, or tendered orally in the presence of two witnesses.

10.3 A resignation which is submitted due to unjustly inflicted grave fear, deceit or substantial error is invalid in canon law and cannot be accepted[85].

10.4 Resignation may be conditional or unconditional.

10.5 The resignation of a cleric takes effect at the moment it is accepted by the Diocesan Bishop[86].

---

[84] Parish priests are requested to offer their resignation to the Diocesan Bishop once they have completed their seventy-fifth year of age, cf can 538§3.

[85] can 188.

[86] The acceptance of the resignation is entirely at the discretion of the Diocesan Bishop, and is not a right of the cleric.

10.6 *For the avoidance of doubt, where a cleric has been invited to withdraw from active ministry pending the resolution of any issue concerning his fitness to serve as a cleric in a particular ecclesiastical office, or to facilitate the conduct of any investigation, any agreement to do so will in no way be a waiver of any acquired right as the holder of that office. Further such a cleric shall not be invited to present his resignation during this period.*

10.7 The secular idea of retirement from employment is not consistent with the theological reality of the ordained ministry. A cleric, although no longer holding a particular office, continues to live the mystery of his order in the service of the Church to the glory of God and remains bound by the rights and duties of his state.

11. Medical Examination and Psychological Assessment

11.1 The Church acknowledges the right of the cleric to privacy[87].

11.2 *Where a cleric is requested to undergo any form of medical examination or psychological assessment it shall be made clear to him in writing:*

(i) *The purpose for which the examination or assessment is required.*

(ii) *The extent to which the examination or assessment may be used to help in determining his fitness for ecclesiastical office and the exercise of his ministry.*

(iii) *The identity of the parties to whom any resultant report is to be provided and the purposes for its production.*

(iv) *The confidentiality which will attach to any resultant report, including the place of storage and the conditions under which it will be divulged.*

(v) *The extent to which the cleric's consent to undergo examination or assessment may represent a waiver of the privilege against self-incrimination.*

---

[87] can 220.

(vi) *The terms upon which the professional has been appointed and the ownership of the document(s) compiled by him.*

(vii) *The cleric's right to a copy of any report.*

11.3 *At no stage shall a cleric be requested to undergo an examination without being informed of the matters contained in paragraph 11.2 and, insofar as these rights have been infringed, the resultant report cannot be used in any canonical process.*

11.4 A cleric cannot be compelled to undergo an examination or assessment and is under no canonical obligation to do so. However, his refusal to comply with a legitimate request of the Diocesan Bishop will mean that this information will not be available to the Diocesan Bishop in coming to a decision concerning the cleric's fitness for ministry and this may have a significant effect on the outcome of any decision.

Part Two:

Processes

12. Confidentiality

12.1 The Code acknowledges the real need for canonical processes to be kept confidential and the right of all parties to safeguard and protect their reputation[88]. Consistent with these principles, all canonical processes are to be treated as confidential.

---

[88] can 220.

13. Removal from Ecclesiastical Office

13.1 Removal from office may arise:

(i) Automatically by virtue of the law itself and subsequently confirmed by decree.

(ii) By decree of the Diocesan Bishop[89] in the exercise of his administrative authority.

13.2 Where a cleric has lost the clerical state, any ecclesiastical office held by him will be lost automatically. The same principle applies to clerics who have publicly defected from the Catholic faith or from the communion of the Church[90], or attempted marriage in contravention of the obligation of celibacy[91]. In these latter cases, it is necessary that the offending conduct and its juridical consequences are the subject of investigation by the Diocesan Bishop and, where the evidence gathered within this process confirms the conduct in question, a declaration issued to that effect. This declaration is merely confirmatory of the automatic consequences which arise by reason of the law itself.

---

[89] cann 192, 193§3.
[90] cf can 1364§.
[91] cf cann 194§1,3°, 277, 1394§1.

13.3 In the case of a secular cleric, whether incardinated into the diocese or not, the power of removal from ecclesiastical office conferred at the discretion of the Diocesan Bishop rests with the Diocesan Bishop[92]. However, prior to issuing the decree, the Diocesan Bishop must be satisfied that there is *just cause* for him to do so[93]. He is required to comply with the provisions of the Code as to the form and content of the decree[94].

13.4 The decree should record in summary the reasons for it and inform the cleric of the right and manner of seeking administrative recourse against the decree.

13.5 The removal of a cleric from an ecclesiastical office may also arise by passage of time, where the appointment was for a determinate period. However, the fact of removal must still be communicated in writing by the competent authority[95].

13.6 *Although not every office within the Church is conferred with the same stability as that of Parish Priest, in the interests of transparency and in order*

---

[92] can 193§3.

[93] Religious clerics may be removed at the discretion of the Diocesan Bishop upon notice being given to the Religious Superior: can 682§2.

[94] cann 48-58.

[95] can 186.

to avoid accusations of arbitrary action on the part of the Diocesan Bishop, it is advisable that the process set out in 14.3, appropriately modified with regards to those consulted, be followed in any case of removal from office[96].

---

[96] The Diocesan Bishop is under no canonical obligation to follow this process in these cases, but such a process is entirely consistent with the canonical rights of due process, cf cann 50, 221.

14. Removal of Parish Priests

14.1 In the case of removal of Parish Priests, the Code provides a detailed process which must be followed by the Diocesan Bishop[97].

14.2 This process may be activated without any wrongdoing on the part of the Parish Priest concerned[98]. The Parish Priest may be removed for the following causes:

 (i) Conduct which causes grave harm or disturbance to the communion of the Church.

 (ii) Ineptitude or infirmity which renders the Parish Priest unable to discharge his function effectively.

 (iii) Loss of good name amongst the community which he serves.

 (iv) Grave neglect or violation of parish duties, which continue despite warning.

 (v) Maladministration of temporal affairs[99].

14.3 In all cases, an allegation relating to one of the above-mentioned causes does not of itself constitute sufficient cause for removal or transfer.

---

[97] can 1740 and following.
[98] can 1740.
[99] can 1741.

The existence of the cause must be established by means of the following process:

(i) **Stage 1:** The conduct of a preliminary investigation by the Diocesan Bishop as to whether a grave cause is present. The process should be documented, with all evidence (both favourable and unfavourable to the priest) recorded. Where it is concluded that the cause arises from the culpability of the priest, this should be recorded. Where, on the other hand, there is no suggestion of culpability on the part of the priest personally, this should be made clear in the record of the investigation and the eventual decree. Throughout the process, the Diocesan Bishop is to be mindful of the need to safeguard the reputation of the cleric concerned.

(ii) **Stage 2:** Having completed the preliminary investigation, the Diocesan Bishop should consult with two Parish Priests drawn from the group established by the Council of Priests[100]. These consultors act as assessors to guide and assist the Diocesan Bishop in the decision he is required to make. The decision, however, is that of the Diocesan Bishop alone.

---

[100] can 1742§1.

(iii) **Stage 3**: *Having considered carefully the views arising from the consultation process, the Diocesan Bishop is to meet with the priest. The purpose of this meeting is to communicate to him the conclusions of the Diocesan Bishop and the evidence upon which the Bishop has relied in support of his own assessment, so that a consensus may be reached, culminating in the priest's resignation from the ecclesiastical office in question. Accordingly, the meeting should be convened at a time and place convenient to both the Bishop and the priest. Moreover, in advance of the meeting the priest should be informed in writing as to:*

a) *The purpose of the meeting.*

b) *The evidence relied upon by the Diocesan Bishop in coming to his decision (including a note of the meeting of the consultors compiled at Stage 2).*

c) *His right to be accompanied at the meeting itself.*

d) *Whether or not the proposed removal has arisen due to culpable conduct on the part of the cleric and, if so, providing details of the conduct itself.*

e) *The details of any replacement ecclesiastical office to which the Diocesan Bishop proposes to appoint the priest, if appropriate.*

(iv) **Stage 4**: *If the priest accepts the decision of the Diocesan Bishop, he is to be given the opportunity to* *confirm his agreement by tendering his resignation[101] from the office in question[102].*

(v) *Where the Diocesan Bishop is satisfied that the priest has received notice of the proposed removal following Stage 2, and has failed to communicate with the Diocesan Bishop despite requests or has expressed an intention not to participate in the process, the Diocesan Bishop is to proceed with the removal, after investigating and excluding the possibility of any extenuating circumstances [103].*

(vi) ***Stage 5:*** *Where the priests opposes the proposed removal, he is to be provided with a reasonable period in order to compile his own case and, where he considers necessary, to gather his own evidence to contradict the material relied upon by the Diocesan Bishop. His response must be put in writing and submitted to the Diocesan Bishop. It is self-evident that the ability of the priest to participate meaningfully in such a process is dependent upon his having been provided with the information relied upon by the Diocesan Bishop, including the proofs (if any) and the written record compiled at Stage 2, together with*

---

[101] Which may be tendered upon a conditional basis - can 1743.

[102] See Section 10 of the Handbook.

[103] can 1744§2.

a written summary of the reasons relied upon by the Diocesan Bishop himself.

(vii) ***Stage 6****: Having received the written submission of the priest, the Diocesan Bishop conducts a review of his earlier decision and again consults with the two Parish Priests[104] involved at Stage 2. If the Diocesan Bishop decides to confirm his earlier decision, he is to issue a decree to that effect. The decree shall include a summary of the reasons for the removal and confirm that the necessary consultation process has taken place. Further, it should expressly draw to the attention of the priest his right to, and manner of seeking, administrative recourse, having particular regard to established time limits.*

(viii) *The Diocesan Bishop shall ensure that the priest is advised of the decision within 30 days of the receipt of the priest's response to the Bishop's findings. The priest shall be informed in writing of any delay and its causes.*

14.4 *Where the removal process ends in the resignation or removal of the priest, no public statement shall be made by the Diocesan Bishop without having first given a written copy of it to the priest concerned*

---

[104] Other Parish Priests may be designated if it is not possible for the same two Parish Priests to take part, cf can 1745,2°.

and providing him with a reasonable opportunity to consider it. If the priest wishes the Bishop to amend it, or otherwise objects to its contents, he must put this in writing. The Bishop shall then consider the request and, where appropriate, amend or vary the statement accordingly. Any period afforded to the priest within this process shall bear in mind the likely desire on the part of the priest to obtain appropriate independent canonical or legal advice.

14.5 Where the process ends with the removal of the priest, he shall cease from exercising the powers attached to the office and take all reasonable steps to assist in the transfer of the office to his successor except when: (i) hierarchical recourse has been initiated and the priest has requested in his petition that the execution of the decree be suspended[105], or (ii) the Diocesan Bishop has himself agreed to the suspension of the decree[106]. In this case the office shall not be regarded as vacant and an administrator shall be appointed.

---

[105] Such a request will be presumed upon the presentation of the petition to the Diocesan Bishop: can 1734.

[106] can 1737§3.

15. Transfer from Ecclesiastical Office

15.1 The request for transfer is an expression of the Diocesan Bishop's ability to properly allocate the resources of the Diocese in a manner best suited to its needs and the common good, a process in which a cleric, under canonical obedience, is required to assist and co-operate.

15.2 Where the Diocesan Bishop seeks to secure the transfer of a cleric against the wishes of the cleric, he must have grounds to do so[107].

15.3 *Where a decision to transfer him meets with resistance on the part of the cleric, the Diocesan Bishop shall convene a meeting with the cleric. The purpose of this meeting is to foster a common mind between the Diocesan Bishop and the cleric in question.*

15.4 *The cleric is to present to the Diocesan Bishop, in writing, the reasons relied upon by him to resist the proposed transfer, together with any supporting documentation. These are to be provided to the*

---

[107] can 190§2. These grounds may vary.

Diocesan Bishop within a reasonable period prior to the holding of the meeting.

15.5 In the event that agreement is not reached concerning the proposed transfer, the Diocesan Bishop retains the right to proceed to issue a decree[108] confirming his decision to transfer the cleric. In accordance with his obligation of obedience, it is incumbent upon the cleric to act in accordance with this decree, whilst safeguarding his right to administrative recourse.

---

[108] In accordance with can 51.

16. Transfer of Parish Priests

16.1 If the good of souls or the necessity or advantage of the Church demand it, the Diocesan Bishop can transfer a priest from one parish to another parish or another office. He is to make this proposal in writing and seek to gain the willing consent of the priest[109].

16.2 If the priest does not agree to the transfer, he is to present to the Diocesan Bishop his reasons for resisting the proposed transfer in writing[110], together with any supporting documentation.

16.3 Having received the submission of the priest, if the Diocesan Bishop still judges that the transfer should proceed, he is to weigh carefully the reasons for and against the transfer with the assistance of two Parish Priests drawn from among the group established by the Council of Priests[111].

16.4 *If he judges that the transfer should still take place, the Diocesan Bishop should convene a meeting with*

---

[109] can 1748.
[110] can 1749.
[111] can 1750.

the priest concerned to explain his reasons and to exhort him to accept the transfer.

16.5 In the event that agreement is not reached concerning the proposed transfer at the meeting, the Diocesan Bishop retains the right to proceed to issue a decree confirming his decision to transfer the priest. In accordance with his obligation of obedience, it is incumbent upon the priest to act in accordance with this decree, whilst safeguarding his right to administrative recourse.

16.6 *The Diocesan Bishop should ensure that the decree expressly addresses:*
   (i) *The decision he has made, together with a summary of reasons relied upon.*
   (ii) *The details of the office to which the priest is to be transferred and the date of the appointment.*
   (iii) *The action required on the part of the priest in order to comply with the decree and the consequences for non-compliance.*
   (iv) *The time limit for compliance, after which the parish will be deemed vacant.*

(v) *The right of the priest to seek redress by means of administrative recourse and the time limit for doing so.*

16.7 Having received notification of the decree, the priest has the right to seek administrative recourse against it as set out in section 20.2.

16.8 *It is strongly recommended that no public statement should be issued concerning the transfer of the priest unless the process referred to in paragraph 14.4 is followed.*

17. Disciplinary Penal Offences and Sanctions

17.1 All communities require and adopt norms of behaviour which seek to regulate the conduct of those who participate in its life and purpose. Such an obvious need is amplified within the ecclesial community since, by its very nature and purpose, it is concerned with the fulfilment of its divine mission and the salvation of souls.

17.2 Not surprisingly, therefore, the Code provides for a catalogue of offences likely to undermine the activity and mission of the Church[112]. These include:

(i) Apostasy, heresy or schism[113].

(ii) Prohibited participation in sacred rites[114].

(iii) Desecration of the sacred species[115].

(iv) The publication of blasphemous or other statements injurious to morals[116].

---

[112] The principal offences are to be found in cann 1364-1399.

[113] can 1364.

[114] can 1365.

[115] can 1367.

[116] can 1369.

Disciplinary Penal Offences and Sanctions 65

- (v) Any form of physical assault against a Diocesan Bishop[117].
- (vi) The use of physical force against a cleric[118].
- (vii) The abuse of ecclesiastical power or office[119].
- (viii) Concubinage or other persist external sexual act which causes scandal[120].
- (ix) A sexual act committed by force, or by threats, or in public, or with a minor[121].
- (x) Failure to comply with a legitimate instruction or request from an ecclesiastical superior including a Diocesan Bishop[122].

17.3 The list set out in the preceding paragraph is in no way intended to be exhaustive and may be supplemented by particular laws promulgated by the Diocesan Bishop.

17.4 As with any community, it is necessary for the Church to provide mechanisms for the purposes of maintaining good order and ecclesiastical discipline,

---

[117] can 1370§2.
[118] can 1370§3.
[119] can 1389.
[120] can 1395§1.
[121] can 1395§2.
[122] can 1371,2°.

particularly when it concerns those who function as sacred ministers of the Church or holders of ecclesiastical office.

17.5 The sanctions adopted by the Church have a unique character[123]. On the one hand they aim at the reparation of scandal and the restoration of justice within the ecclesial community (expiatory penalties[124]), but also seek the conversion of the offender (medicinal penalties[125]).

---

[123] can 1341.
[124] can 1336.
[125] cann 1331-1333.

18. Disciplinary Penal Process

18.1 By incorporation through baptism[126], all of the faithful have the obligation to maintain communion with the Church[127].

18.2 Equally, and no matter what the state or condition of the individual concerned (whether clerical or lay), each enjoys a number of substantive and procedural rights in connection with the disciplinary processes of the Church, they include:

(i) The right not to be subjected to any form of disciplinary sanction save as provided for by law[128].

(ii) The right to be heard prior to any such sanction being imposed[129].

(iii) The right to be represented within any disciplinary or other judicial process[130].

(iv) The right for the penal provision to be strictly interpreted[131].

---

[126] can 96.

[127] can 209.

[128] can 221§3.

[129] can 1720,1° and in the case of sanctions imposed by decree see can 50.

[130] can 1723. In default of appointment by the cleric concerned, the Judge is under an obligation to do so.

[131] can 18.

18.3 Since the detail of the offences themselves is addressed within the Code and section 17 of this Directory, it is sufficient to note that the Church attaches particular gravity to a number of offences. Certain offences and the competence to adjudicate upon them have been reserved to the Holy See itself[132]. In such cases, reference should be made to the relevant *motu proprio* and specific norms promulgated therein in connection with these "reserved matters". Such reserved offences include:

(i) Simulation of the Eucharist.

(ii) Desecration of the Sacred Species.

(iii) Sexual impropriety involving minors.

(iv) Direct and indirect violation of the seal of confession.

(v) Concelebrating the Eucharist with ministers not in communion with the Roman Pontiff.

18.4 What follows should be taken as a general overview of the penal process insofar as it relates to clerics. It represents the key stages of the disciplinary penal process in respect of those matters not otherwise provided for in the Code or reserved to the Holy See.

---

[132] Such offences have been reserved mainly to the Congregation for the Doctrine of the Faith (CDF). See Apostolic Constitution, *Pastor Bonus*, 28th June 1988, art 52, and Apostolic Letter MP, *Sacramentorum sanctitatis tutela*, 30th April 2001.

Disciplinary Penal Process

Preliminary Investigation [Stage 1]

18.5 The penal process may be activated and penalties applied only insofar as canon law allows[133]. Wrongdoing *per se* is not sufficient. It must also be shown that the conduct of which complaint is made represents an external commission of an offence which is gravely imputable[134]. Having received information or an allegation which has at least the semblance of truth, the Diocesan Bishop, or his delegate[135], must first investigate the nature and circumstances of the offence and whether the accused is implicated in the commission of the offence itself. He must open this preliminary investigation by means of a decree.

18.6 Following the gathering of this evidence it is for the Diocesan Bishop himself to consider (i) whether it is likely that an offence has been committed; (ii)

---

[133] can 221§3.

[134] Imputability refers to the subjective aspect of the offence, i.e. that it was committed voluntarily, consciously and freely. Imputability can arise from malice (the deliberate violation of a law or precept) or culpability (the omission of due diligence), cf can 1321§1.

[135] The delegate, who possesses the same rights and duties as an auditor within a canonical process, can in principle be either clerical or lay (can 1428§2). However, given the requirement of clerical personnel for a judicial process and the stipulation that in cases which could involve the reputation of a priest the notary must be a priest (can 483§2), it may be considered more appropriate that the delegate be a priest, depending on the nature of the allegation. In any event, the appointment should be confirmed in writing and the remit of the authority defined.

whether the accused is implicated in the commission of the offence; and (iii) whether having regard to all of the circumstances, it is necessary or appropriate to respond by way of process to impose a penalty through penal trial or administrative decree[136].

18.7 Throughout this process the Diocesan Bishop and those acting on his behalf must ensure that the reputation of those involved (e.g. accuser and accused) are not placed at risk of harm[137]. For this and other reasons:

(i) All documents arising out of this process must be maintained under the strictest confidentiality[138].

(ii) *All communications arising out of or in connection with the process, and indeed the process itself, must be confidential and shall not be subject to any public statement concerning the nature, cause or status of the investigation, without the consent of the accused person.*

(iii) *Any delegate or other agent of the Diocesan Bishop involved in the conduct of the preliminary investigation who fails to act in accordance with such confidentiality shall be subject to penalty.*

---

[136] can 1718.
[137] can 1717§2.
[138] can 1719.

18.8 *The conduct of a preliminary investigation, in terms of both its scope and duration, is to be regulated by reasonableness. In the conduct of this stage of the process therefore particular regard shall be had to the following principles:*

(i) *The preliminary investigation is not intended to constitute the trial of the alleged offence. Rather, it is concerned only with whether there is a case which the accused is required to answer and a judicial or administrative process embarked upon.*

(ii) *In the interests of justice, the gathering of evidence shall also include evidence likely to exonerate the accused.*

(iii) *The duration and scope of the investigation must be assessed by reference to the facts of each case. Clearly, reasonableness and proportionality will have different meanings depending upon the detail and timing of the alleged misconduct.*

(iv) *Given the preliminary nature of the investigation, special care should be taken to ensure that the guilt of the accused has not been determined nor that there can be any suggestion of the process having been concluded at this stage. It is the possibility that there has been misconduct which is being explored, not actual misconduct.*

18.9 *Whilst the preliminary investigation is not a preliminary trial of the accused, every effort shall be made to inform the accused as to:*

(i) *The fact that an investigation has been commenced.*

(ii) *The nature of the allegation which has been raised against him.*

(iii) *The identity of the parties instructed to carry out the investigation and the date upon which authority was delegated to them.*

(iv) *The likely timescale of the preliminary investigation and the point at which it is anticipated that the Diocesan Bishop will be in a position to communicate his decision to the accused.*

(v) *The privilege against self incrimination.*

(vi) *The rights and obligations of the accused during the investigation including, but not limited to, his right to continued financial support from the Diocesan Bishop and the provisions to be made for his welfare and accommodation.*

18.10 *Notice of such a process may generate a time of exceptional personal distress and confusion for the accused cleric. Accordingly, it is of the highest importance that there is both clarity and transparency of communications passing between* *the Diocesan Bishop and the cleric concerned. To this end, the following practice should be observed:*

(i) *The cleric shall have the right to be accompanied at any meetings to be held between the cleric and the Diocesan Bishop and/or the delegate of the Diocesan Bishop.*

(ii) *At any meeting between the cleric and the Diocesan Bishop and/or his delegate a detailed minute shall be taken recording the terms, purpose and content of the meeting. Following the meeting the written minute shall be circulated to the cleric and his advisor for their agreement. In the event that there is disagreement as to the content or accuracy of the document, necessary amendments shall be noted and recorded in the document and signed by all parties present.*

(iii) *Where the nature of the information or allegation requires the reporting of the information to any statutory or other body, a detailed record shall be maintained of the date, purpose and terms of this communication together with the name of the person communicating the information.*

Conclusion of the Preliminary Investigation [Stage 2]

18.11 After gathering the evidence, if, in the opinion of the Diocesan Bishop, there is material to suggest that a reserved offence may have been committed, he shall submit all of the proofs and related documents to the Congregation for the Doctrine of the Faith.

18.12 In all other cases in which the Diocesan Bishop enjoys competence and where he has concluded that there is material indicating the commission of a canonical offence in which the accused is implicated, he shall:

(i) Determine whether it is desirable or necessary for the matter to be the subject of some form of canonical process.

(ii) Consider whether it is desirable to proceed by way of penal trial or administrative decree[139].

(iii) Issue a decree, which must be notified to the accused, confirming the conclusion of the preliminary investigation and its outcome[140].

Extrajudicial Decree [Stage 3]

18.13 Where the Diocesan Bishop is satisfied there is just cause[141] and the universal law permits him to do

---

[139] Although it is for the Diocesan Bishop to decide whether to proceed by way of penal trial or extrajudicial decree, the preference of the Code in penal cases is a judicial trial, cf can 1342§1. In cases which may involve the imposition and declaration of perpetual penalties or when the law or precept itself requires it, a penal trial must always be initiated, cf can 1342§2.

[140] can 1718.

[141] can 1342.

Disciplinary Penal Process

so[142], he may proceed by way of decree rather than penal trial.

18.14 If the Diocesan Bishop chooses to proceed in this way, he shall:

(i) Notify the accused of the detail of the case presented against him, together with the supporting evidence.

(ii) Provide the accused with a reasonable period in which to prepare his defence to the allegations.

(iii) *Advise the accused of the privilege against self-incrimination.*

(iv) Advise the accused of his right to canonical representation and in the event that the accused does not appoint one, appoint one *ex officio.*

(v) Fully consider the material and submissions relied upon by the accused and the fact that the material presented against him has not been challenged by appropriate questioning or other process.

(vi) Issue a decree detailing his judgment, the reasons for it and the evidence upon which he relied, and the penalties imposed or declared.

(vii) The accused shall be informed of his right to, and the manner of seeking, administrative recourse, with particular reference to the established time limits.

---

[142] can 1718§1,3°.

18.15 In all other respects, the form of the decree issued by the Diocesan Bishop shall comply with the provisions of the Code[143].

Commencement of the Penal Trial [Stage 4]

18.16 Where the Bishop is satisfied that there is evidence which suggests the commission of a canonical offence[144], the proper response to which is the imposition of some form of canonical penalty, and either the law requires the conduct of a penal trial, or, there is no justification for proceeding by way of administrative decree, he must initiate a penal trial. He must issue a decree to this effect.

18.17 Having issued this decree the following process shall be followed:

(i) The Diocesan Bishop is to transmit all of the material gathered during the Preliminary Investigation to the Promoter of Justice[145].

(ii) A Judge will be appointed to hear the case[146]. The Judge must be a cleric and, where the matter may

---

[143] cann 48-58 and can 1342.

[144] Other than one which is not reserved to the Holy See.

[145] can 1721.

[146] Observing the norms of cann 1447-8. Where the subject matter relates to can 1395§2 the Judges should preferably be selected from outside the diocesan jurisdiction of the Diocesan Bishop.

lead to dismissal from the clerical state, the case must be heard and determined by a collegiate tribunal of three Judges[147], each of whom shall be a cleric.

(iii) The Promoter draws up a formal petition outlining the conduct of which complaint is made, the parties implicated and the evidence relied upon[148].

(iv) Upon receipt of the petition, the Judge shall issue a decree confirming his acceptance of the petition and summoning the accused to trial[149]. A copy of the petition, containing a clear statement of the offences alleged, is to be attached to the decree.

(v) Following representations from the accused and the Promoter the Judge or President of the Collegiate Tribunal shall by decree identify the questions requiring resolution and determination[150] and provide a timetable for the provision of proofs and related evidence[151].

Conduct of the Penal Trial [Step 5]

18.18 Within the conduct of a Penal Trial, the following principles shall be observed:

---

[147] can 1425§1.
[148] can 1504.
[149] can 1507.
[150] can 1513.
[151] can 1516.

(i) The burden of proving the commission of an offence rests with the Promoter[152].

(ii) The Judge(s) are entitled to question the parties and, indeed, may be requested by the parties to conduct such questioning[153].

(iii) *Whilst a party may be required to answer questions posed, the accused is entitled to, and is to be reminded of, the privilege against self-incrimination. No adverse inference is to be drawn from a refusal to incriminate himself.*

(iv) Evidence is to be given on oath[154], except that given by the accused[155].

(v) Unless there is evidence to the contrary, public documents will be assumed to be valid[156] and proof of the facts contained within them.

(vi) Neither party shall be required to produce evidence or documentation where to do so would infringe canonical secrecy[157].

(vii) Witnesses must be examined before the tribunal unless the Judge(s) consider otherwise[158]. The

---

[152] can 1526§1.
[153] can 1530.
[154] can 1532.
[155] can 1728§2.
[156] can 1541.
[157] can 1546§1.
[158] can 1558.

Disciplinary Penal Process 79

       advocate of the accused, but not the accused himself, may be present at the examination[159].

(viii) Having heard the parties, the Judge(s) may consider it opportune to visit a place or inspect something connected with the case[160].

(ix) When all the evidence has been gathered, the parties and advocates shall be permitted to inspect the documentation gathered by the tribunal and may adduce additional proofs concerning the matters contained within them[161].

(x) The accused and the Promotor are to make written submissions concerning the determination of the case[162], with the accused or his advocate always having the right to write or speak last[163].

(xi) The standard of proof by which a case is to be decided is that of moral certitude[164].

(xii) Upon conclusion of the trial the Judge(s) will issue a formal judgment detailing the judgment reached, the reasons for the conclusion and the consequences for the parties and their respective rights[165].

---

[159] can 1559.

[160] Having followed the procedure in can 1582.

[161] can 1598.

[162] In exceptional cases, this may take place orally – can 1602.

[163] can 1725.

[164] can 1608§1.

[165] can 1612.

18.19 Any person who considers himself aggrieved by any sentence has the right to appeal[166]. The accused shall within the course of the judgment be advised of his right of appeal, the appropriate forum for determining the appeal and the time limit within which the right of appeal must be exercised[167].

18.20 An appeal will have the effect of suspending any penalty or sanction imposed upon the accused[168].

---

[166] can 1628.
[167] cann 1633 - 1634.
[168] can 1638.

19. Temporary Withdrawal from Active Ministry

19.1 The Code does not recognise any right on the part of the Diocesan Bishop to "suspend" a cleric from active ministry pending any form of investigations, other than during the course of a penal trial[169]. Thus, there is no provision in the Code for what has come to be called "administrative leave".

19.2 *Nonetheless, there are occasions during an investigation when there is a need to prevent scandal, protect the freedom of witnesses and to safeguard the course of justice, and so a temporary withdrawal from active ministry is necessary.*

19.3 *Where temporary withdrawal from active ministry is deemed necessary by the Diocesan Bishop, the first step should always be to seek such a withdrawal on a voluntary basis.*

19.4 *Only if voluntary withdrawal cannot be achieved should the Diocesan Bishop resort to disciplinary*

---

[169] A cleric may only be prohibited from the exercise of ministry once a penal trial has been initiated, can 1722.

measures in accordance with the provisions of the Code to limit the ministerial activity of the cleric. These measures must be imposed by way of precept[170].

19.5 *In all cases, the cleric concerned is entitled to the following:*

(i) *a statement of the decision in writing.*

(ii) *the reason for the request or requirement to withdraw from active ministry.*

(iii) *a statement that the withdrawal is a neutral act.*

(iv) *legal and canonical representation.*

(v) *details of agreements regarding what information to be placed in the public domain.*

(vi) *confirmation that temporary withdrawal from active ministry does not constitute removal from office.*

(vii) *information regarding remuneration and residence during the time of withdrawal.*

(viii) *an initial review date of the situation.*

19.6 *When temporary withdrawal takes place as a result of an allegation involving the safeguarding of children and vulnerable adults, the cleric has all the*

---

[170] In issuing a precept, the Diocesan Bishop shall proceed in accordance with Section 8 of this Directory.

entitlements listed in 19.5. In addition, the following must be observed:

(i) *With regards to clause (ii), the individual is entitled to know that an allegation has been received, and that it is an allegation relating to the safeguarding of children or vulnerable adults. However, the details cannot be passed on at this point and it is necessary for close liaison to take place between the diocesan and statutory authorities to ensure that information passed to the subject of the allegation does not interfere with a police investigation process.*

(ii) *The individual is to be given a copy of the Covenant of Care setting out the details of the restrictions placed on him during temporary withdrawal, as drawn up by the Safeguarding Co-ordinator/Officer and approved by the Diocesan Bishop.*

19.7 Where temporary withdrawal from active ministry is either not possible or inappropriate, the Diocesan Bishop may consider taking the following disciplinary measures:

(i) For a cleric who holds no ecclesiastical office in the diocese, any previously delegated faculties may be administratively removed[171], while any *de*

---

[171] cann 391§1, 132§1, 142§1.

lege faculties may be removed or restricted by the competent authority as provided in the law[172].

(ii) He may also judge that the circumstances surrounding a particular case constitute a "good and reasonable cause" for a priest to celebrate the Eucharist with no member of the faithful present[173].

(iii) He may regulate the rights of the cleric in accordance with canon 223§2.

19.8 Temporary withdrawal from active ministry must be carefully distinguished from the canonical penalty of suspension.

---

[172] e.g. can 764.
[173] can 906.

20. Administrative Recourse

20.1 A cleric who considers that, in issuing an administrative or disciplinary decree, the Diocesan Bishop has acted unlawfully, arbitrarily or unjustly is entitled to seek redress by way of administrative recourse[174].

20.2 Where he wishes to challenge the terms of a decree the following process must be followed:

(i) Within 10 days[175] he must petition the Diocesan Bishop in writing to reconsider his decision.

(ii) It is presumed that the petition includes a request for the suspension of the effects of the decree in those matters where the suspension does not take place by the law itself[176].

---

[174] can 1733 and following.

[175] can 1734§1.

[176] can 1736. An extrajudicial decree imposing or declaring a sanction or penalty is automatically suspended (can 1353). In the case of a decree concerning the removal or transfer of a Parish Priest, the suspension means that a new Parish Priest cannot be appointed during recourse. However, the priest concerned must abstain from the exercise of his office, vacate the presbytery and hand over everything pertaining to the parish to the parochial administrator (cann 1747, 1752).

(iii) The Diocesan Bishop, having considered the request, may issue a further decree amending or revoking the earlier one, or confirm the rejection of the request[177].

(iv) Where the request lodged with the Diocesan Bishop remains unanswered for the period of 30 days, the Diocesan Bishop shall be deemed to have refused the request and hierarchical recourse can be pursued[178] within 15 days[179].

(v) Where the request results in the issue of a further decree rejecting the request, the cleric has the right to petition the Holy See by way of hierarchical recourse within 15 days[180].

(vi) The Holy See has the right to confirm, change or revoke the decree[181].

---

[177] can 1735.
[178] can 1735.
[179] can 1737§2.
[180] can 1737§2.
[181] can 1739.

21. Dispute Resolution

21.1 The Code encourages those within the Church to seek to avoid contentious disputes wherever possible[182] and urges the faithful to refer the subject matter of any dispute to arbitration.[183]

21.2 It must be recognised that issues can and do arise in connection with perceptions of mistreatment and apparent lack of concern or support in relationships between the clergy themselves and between the clergy and their bishop. However, whenever they arise, every effort should be made to ensure that concerns are in the first instance resolved informally between the parties involved. Where, either by reason of the subject matter of the grievance or of the identity of the persons concerned, this is unlikely to bear fruit, formal canonical processes such as administrative recourse may be embarked upon, having due regard for determined canonical time limits.

---

[182] can 1446.
[183] can 1713.

21.3 *In the first instance, any grievance should be directed to the Diocesan Bishop by means of the following process:*

(i) *The cleric shall put his grievance in writing, providing sufficient detail to enable the Diocesan Bishop to identify both the nature of the grievance and the matters said to have given rise to it. If appropriate, the cleric should identify the redress he considers necessary to resolve the grievance.*

(ii) *The Diocesan Bishop is to respond formally to the grievance within 7 days.*

(iii) *Following receipt of the grievance, the Diocesan Bishop shall invite the cleric to attend a formal meeting. This invitation should confirm the confidential nature of the process and the right of the cleric to be accompanied during the course of the process. If there are circumstances which preclude the swift resolution of the grievance, these should be identified and, where possible, a strategy proposed for resolution.*

(iv) *The Diocesan Bishop should aim to conclude the grievance process within a reasonable period of time avoiding any unnecessary delay likely to compound the sense of grievance expressed by the cleric. The Diocesan Bishop should keep the cleric fully informed as to the manner in which he proposes to deal with the grievance and its progress.*

(v) *All communications between the cleric and the Diocesan Bishop shall be put in writing. Similarly any meeting shall be recorded in writing and the minutes approved by both.*

(vi) *At the conclusion of the grievance process, the Diocesan Bishop is to notify the cleric of the outcome. This must be done in writing, detailing the conclusion reached and the reasons for it.*

21.4 *If on conclusion of the grievance process the cleric remains dissatisfied, depending on the nature of the grievance, it remains open to him to pursue his rights by means of the processes mentioned in 20.1.*

21.5 *Where the pursuit of a grievance is considered by either party to be impractical, the cleric and the Diocesan Bishop may agree that the dispute shall be referred to a mediator, chosen from a panel established by the Conference. Where this is the case, it shall be recorded in writing detailing the nature of the dispute and the parties' agreement to refer the matter to mediation or non-binding adjudication.*

21.6 *The mediator appointed shall have the power to:*

(i) *Express opinions and provide advice as to the respective rights and obligations of the parties.*

(ii) *Make recommendations to both parties as to the manner in which the dispute may be resolved consistent with canon law.*

21.7 *Whilst it is the function of the mediator to assist in the resolution of the dispute, he shall have no jurisdiction or competence to issue any binding adjudication upon either party or require either party to take action affecting their canonical rights.*

21.8 *The mediation shall be conducted in the spirit of compromise and under confidentiality with the result that nothing arising during the process may be used within any subsequent judicial process.*

21.9 *The panel of mediators shall consist of persons having suitable qualifications and expertise to participate in the process and, as far as possible, they should not be subject to any potential legal, juridical, professional or personal conflict. Therefore, the mediator should not be selected from the diocese of the Diocesan Bishop concerned.*

21.10 *Mediation cannot be used for any dispute arising out of or in connection with the conduct or conclusion of any penal or disciplinary process or the legislative authority of the Diocesan Bishop.*

21.11 *The parties may refer any dispute to mediation whether before or after embarking upon any other process, provided that in the latter instance, the proceedings shall by agreement be stayed so as to provide a reasonable period for the appointment of a mediator and the conduct of the mediation.*

Appendix 1: Definition of Terms

Cleric A man who has validly received ordination to the diaconate and/or priesthood.

Decree In this document, a formal document issued by the Diocesan Bishop or someone authorised on his behalf which has the effect of defining, restricting or limiting the rights of the cleric or the manner in which he may conduct himself. Any such decree shall record by whom it has been issued, a brief summary of the reasons for its issue and the action, if any, required of the cleric in order to secure compliance. Such a decree will often have the nature of a singular precept in canon law[184].

Diocese A portion of the people of God, entrusted to the care of the Diocesan Bishop[185].

Diocesan Bishop A Bishop to whom a portion of the people of God has been entrusted and who exercises the executive, judicial and legislative governance of a Diocese[186].

---

[184] can 49.
[185] can 369.
[186] can 381.

Appendix 1: Definition of Terms

Holy See The Supreme Pontiff and/or all other institutes of the Roman Curia[187].

Incardination The lifelong bond created between the cleric and a Particular Church[188] which arises upon ordination or, in exceptional cases, following transfer between one Particular Church and another[189]. This bond also arises between clerical religious institutes, clerical societies of apostolic life[190] or personal prelatures and clerics who belong to them.

Particular Church Within this document refers primarily to the Diocese.

Parish Priest A priest to whom the full and stable pastoral care of a parish has been entrusted under the authority of the Diocesan Bishop.[191]

The Code The Code of Canon Law 1983.

The Conference The Catholic Bishops' Conference of England and Wales.

---

[187] can 361.
[188] can 265.
[189] cann 267, 268.
[190] can 736§1.
[191] can 519.

Appendix 2:
Checklist for Diocesan Handbooks

The following issues should be dealt with in more detail by particular legislation:

Incardination

Retreats

Sabbaticals

On-going formation and development

Rest periods

Financial provision

Medical Care

Welfare of sick clergy

Provision for those no longer holding Office

Accommodation